Kilmanns Personality Style Instrument

RALPH H. KILMANN
AND ASSOCIATES

Distributed by
KILMANN DIAGNOSTICS
1 Suprema Drive
Newport Coast, CA 92657
www.kilmanndiagnostics.com
info@kilmanndiagnostics.com
949.497.8766

PERSONALITY STYLE INSTRUMENT

Introduction

People respond differently to what goes on in their organization: They have different styles of interacting with others and ways of getting their work done. It is not as if one approach is necessarily better than another, but rather that one person's style is simply *different* from another's. This instrument merely tries to pinpoint the distinctive ways in which you choose to respond to people and events in your organization.

Response Scale

Carefully study the response scale below. You will be asked to use the numbers on this scale to record your responses to the forty items in this instrument. You may refer back to this page at any time.

0   *I never* experience the situation in the manner depicted. In fact, it is difficult for me to relate to the kind of response described.

1   *I occasionally* experience the situation in the manner depicted. It does not happen often, but I can identify with the kind of response described.

2   *I frequently* experience the situation in the manner depicted. It is a typical response, even though I do react differently sometimes.

3   *I constantly* experience the situation in the manner depicted. Very rarely do I respond differently.

4   *I always* experience the situation in the manner depicted. I cannot imagine reacting differently.

PERSONALITY STYLE INSTRUMENT

Instructions

On the next pages, you will find forty questions that ask if you react in certain ways in work-related situations. For each item, circle the number that best captures your typical style. Even if the response categories (0 to 4) do not perfectly capture the relative frequency of your reactions, still circle the number that comes closest to your most natural tendency.

Never—Frequently—Always

← →

		Never				Always
1.	Do you prefer to base your decisions on established facts (rather than on abstract ideas)?	0	1	2	3	4
2.	Do you enjoy working with people who continually present new ideas?	0	1	2	3	4
3.	Do you enjoy helping newly hired employees "get on board" and "learn the ropes?"	0	1	2	3	4
4.	Do you wonder about the real value of your organization to society?	0	1	2	3	4

PERSONALITY STYLE INSTRUMENT

⟵————————————⟶

5. Do you prefer having a boss with "two feet on the ground?"

0   1   2   3   4

6. Do you prefer using logical analysis when working on a problem?

0   1   2   3   4

7. Do you enjoy attending company functions and social events?

0   1   2   3   4

8. Do you lose interest in projects that do not seem to contribute much to your organization's mission?

0   1   2   3   4

9. Do you prefer to solve day-to-day problems (versus developing long-term strategies)?

0   1   2   3   4

10. Do you enjoy thinking about future possibilities for your organization?

0   1   2   3   4

11. At meetings, do you find it easy to communicate your feelings and emotions to others?

0   1   2   3   4

PERSONALITY STYLE INSTRUMENT

Never—Frequently—Always

← →

12. At meetings, do you wish others would share their inner values and personal beliefs more openly?

   0   *1*   *2*   *3*   *4*

13. Do you judge your peers according to who has the most relevant work experience or job knowledge?

   0   *1*   *2*   *3*   *4*

14. Do you find yourself organizing themes into categories, diagrams, or frameworks?

   0   *1*   *2*   *3*   *4*

15. Do you enjoy socializing—after hours—with your coworkers?

   0   *1*   *2*   *3*   *4*

16. Do you look forward to working on projects that deal with the future welfare of your organization?

   0   *1*   *2*   *3*   *4*

17. Do you prefer work assignments that are provided with clear and specific guidelines?

   0   *1*   *2*   *3*   *4*

PERSONALITY STYLE INSTRUMENT

Never—Frequently—Always

$\longleftrightarrow$

18. Do you prefer developing new solutions to work problems (versus applying the usual approach)?

    0   *1*   *2*   *3*   *4*

19. When making decisions, are you especially concerned about the likes and dislikes of the people affected?

    0   *1*   *2*   *3*   *4*

20. Do you prefer to dress as you like (versus dressing according to the accepted manner)?

    0   *1*   *2*   *3*   *4*

21. Do you prefer finding the available facts in the situation (versus brainstorming the possibilities)?

    0   *1*   *2*   *3*   *4*

22. Do you look for trends, patterns, and recurring themes when examining work-related problems?

    0   *1*   *2*   *3*   *4*

23. Do you expect a manager to be especially people oriented and very sensitive to people's needs?

    0   *1*   *2*   *3*   *4*

PERSONALITY STYLE INSTRUMENT

Never—Frequently—Always

24. Do you wonder about the fate of your company (versus getting the daily work done)?

0	1	2	3	4

25. Do you expect others to conform to established work procedures (versus proceeding according to personal preferences)?

0	1	2	3	4

26. Do you like analyzing theories that try to explain why people (and things) work the way they do?

0	1	2	3	4

27. Do you get pleasure from being courteous to your coworkers?

0	1	2	3	4

28. Do you worry whether groups and departments are cooperating enough with one another?

0	1	2	3	4

29. Do you prefer a job with precisely defined goals and objectives?

0	1	2	3	4

PERSONALITY STYLE INSTRUMENT

Never—Frequently—Always

⟵——————————⟶

30. Do you enjoy investigating how new work technologies will affect the future of all organizations?

    0   *1*   *2*   *3*   *4*

31. Do you like it when your coworkers stop by to chat with you?

    0   *1*   *2*   *3*   *4*

32. Do you find yourself daydreaming about making a major contribution to your organization or society?

    0   *1*   *2*   *3*   *4*

33. Do you work very hard to get all the details right—to dot all the "i"s and cross all the "t"s?

    0   *1*   *2*   *3*   *4*

34. Do you prefer a coworker who develops new approaches (versus implementing practical solutions)?

    0   *1*   *2*   *3*   *4*

35. When new corporate policies or work procedures are announced, do you wonder how certain people will feel and react?

    0   *1*   *2*   *3*   *4*

PERSONALITY STYLE INSTRUMENT

36. Do you admire the people who articulate the long-term vision or strategic goal of your organization?

0   1   2   3   4

37. Are you concerned about the wasted time and effort that occurs because people do not follow established rules and work procedures?

0   1   2   3   4

38. Would you like to spend more of your time developing innovative products or services for your organization?

0   1   2   3   4

39. Do you like developing friendships with those in your work group?

0   1   2   3   4

40. Do you find personal meaning in the general mission of your organization?

0   1   2   3   4

Scoring Your Responses

In the spaces below, please transfer all the numbers that you circled on the previous pages. Then add up each column as shown. The resulting sums are your scores for four personality styles—ST, NT, SF, and NF—which will be explained shortly.

1. ___	2. ___	3. ___	4. ___
5. ___	6. ___	7. ___	8. ___
9. ___	10. ___	11. ___	12. ___
13. ___	14. ___	15. ___	16. ___
17. ___	18. ___	19. ___	20. ___
21. ___	22. ___	23. ___	24. ___
25. ___	26. ___	27. ___	28. ___
29. ___	30. ___	31. ___	32. ___
33. ___	34. ___	35. ___	36. ___
37. ___	38. ___	39. ___	40. ___

Sum:	Sum:	Sum:	Sum:
ST	**NT**	**SF**	**NF**

Graphing Your Scores

On the opposite page, please record each of your four scores in the corner space by its corresponding personality style.

Then, for each of your four scores, plot the number along the diagonal in its quadrant. For example, if your ST score is 24, you would circle the hash mark in the ST quadrant portraying this number. If your NT score is 36, you would circle the hash mark in the NT quadrant representing this number, and so on.

Once you have plotted all four of your scores on the graph, connect all four points. The resulting four-sided shape is a **quadrangle**. It will be used to signify whether you are a "generalist" or a "specialist" in the way you respond to various work-related situations.

PERSONALITY STYLE INSTRUMENT

My Personality Profile

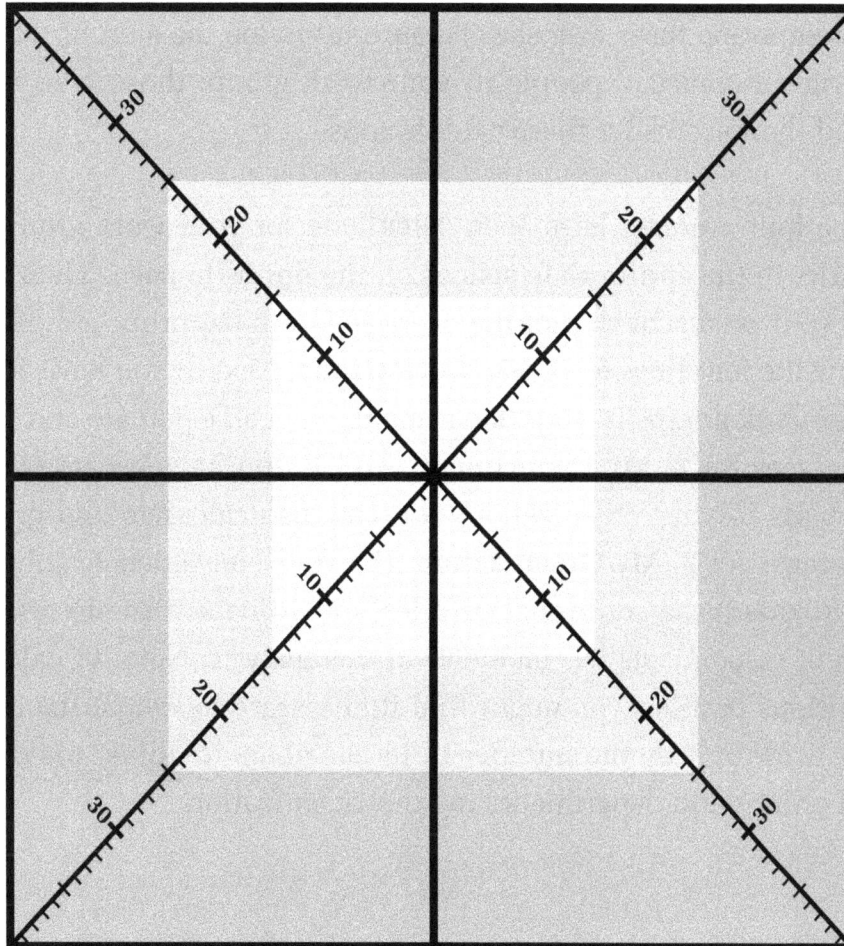

ST SCORE

NT SCORE

SF SCORE

NF SCORE

Developing Organizational Profiles

Once all the people in your group have obtained their scores on the four personality styles, collect their numbers together on a separate sheet of paper so you can calculate four averages: one for ST, NT, SF, and NF. While computing these averages, be sure to divide the sum of the scores by the right number of people in your work group: those who actually provided their scores for these calculations.

Once the four averages have been calculated for your work group, enter the results in the appropriate spaces on the opposite page. Then, as you did for your own scores, plot the averages on the appropriate diagonals and draw the four lines for **1. My Work Group**. Next, if you have access to the other work groups in your department, you can calculate and plot the four averages for **2. My Department**. And if you have access to all the departments in your organization, you can also calculate and graph the four averages for **3. My Organization**. For your convenience, subsequent pages provide these additional profiles, including a space to record the number of respondents (N) included in the analysis. Note: In calculating these various profiles, you might find it necessary to weight the averages of each work unit by the number of its members to adjust for different sizes of groups and departments in your organization.

PERSONALITY STYLE INSTRUMENT

1. My Work Group (N = _____)

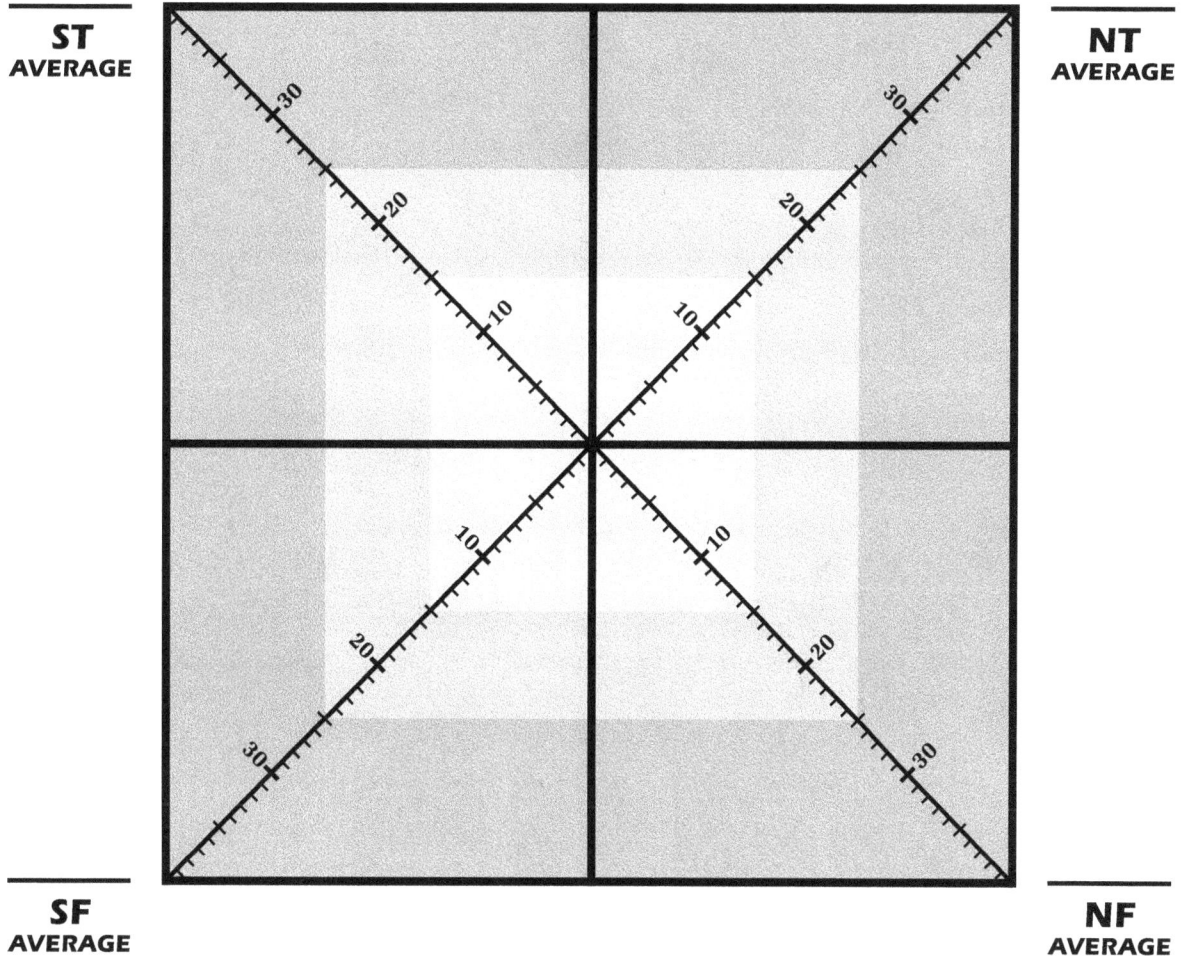

2. My Department (N = _____)

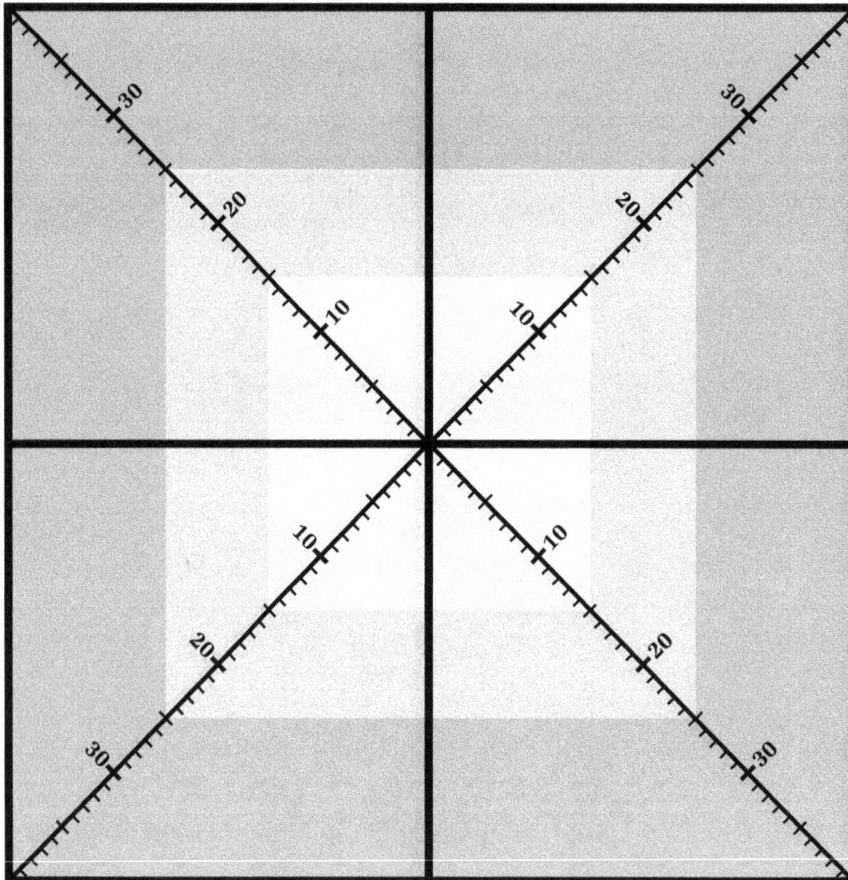

ST
AVERAGE

NT
AVERAGE

SF
AVERAGE

NF
AVERAGE

3. My Organization (N = _____)

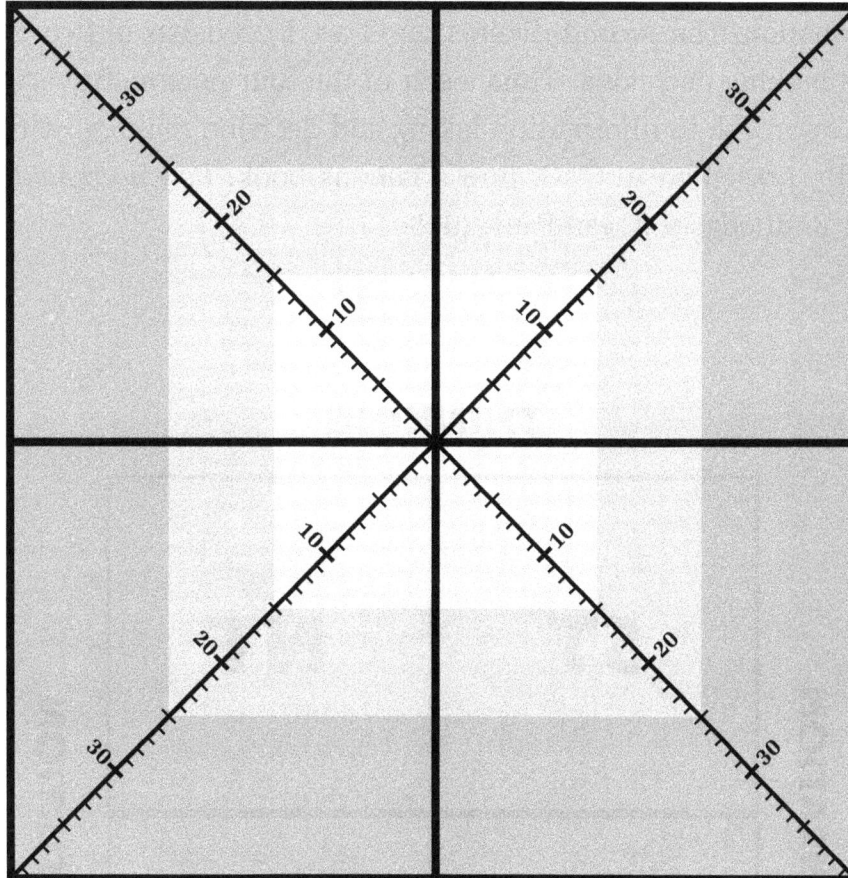

ST AVERAGE

NT AVERAGE

SF AVERAGE

NF AVERAGE

Defining Four Personality Styles

As shown below, the four personality styles are a composite of two key distinctions: Sensation (S) vs. Intuition (N) and Thinking (T) vs. Feeling (F). The first distinction (S vs. N) consists of two different ways of taking in information. The second distinction (T vs. F) consists of two different ways of making decisions. Thus, each of the four personality styles is a unique approach to information taking and decision making, which was originally presented in C. G. Jung's famous book: *Psychological Types.* Boston: Routledge & Kegan Paul, 1923.

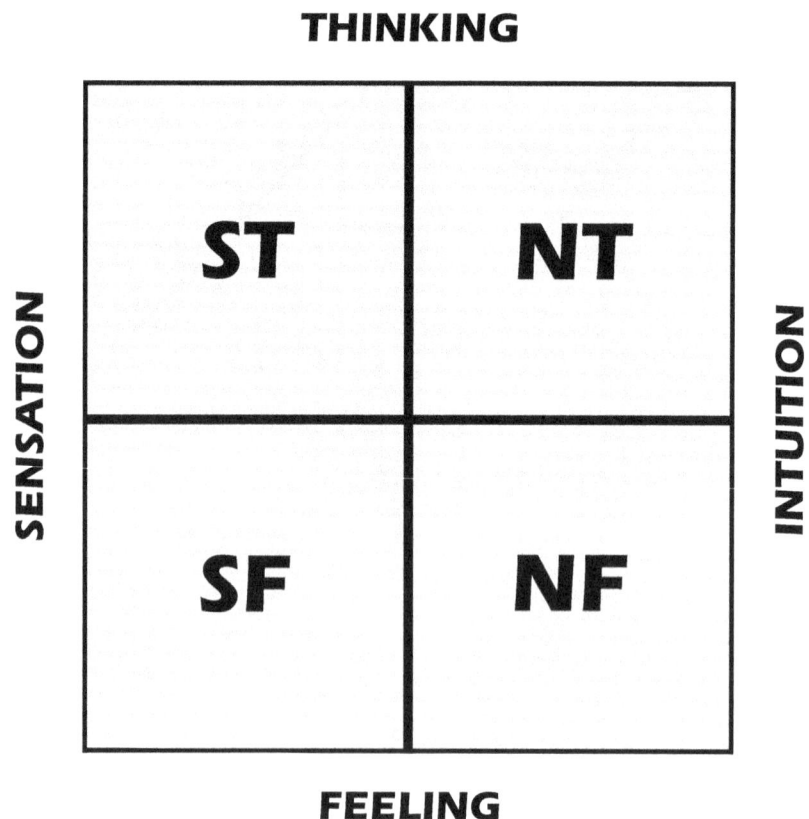

THINKING

ST	**NT**
SF	**NF**

SENSATION (left side)   **INTUITION** (right side)

FEELING

There are two ways in which people take in information: sensation and intuition. Sensation refers to the preference for taking in information by the five senses. It focuses on the details, facts, and **specifics** of a situation: what can be seen, touched, smelled, and so forth. In contrast, intuition is a preference for the **whole** rather than the parts, for the new possibilities, hunches, and future implications of any subject—what cannot be seen or touched directly. People develop a preference for one or the other mode of taking in information. Even though they can use either sensation or intuition when required, they may be unable to apply each equally well. The information-taking mode that is not preferred, in fact, is regarded as a person's weaker function or "blind side."

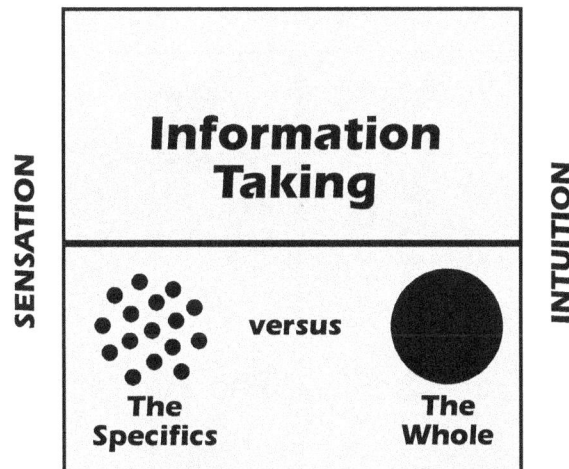

There are two basic ways in which people arrive at decisions: thinking and feeling. Thinking is an impersonal, logical, analytical preference for making a decision: using the **head.** If such and such is true, then this and that follow, as based on a logical analysis. Feeling, in contrast, refers to a personal, subjective, or unique way of making a decision: using the **heart.** Does the person like the alternative? Does it fit with his (or her) values and self-image? While arriving at such a conclusion is not logical per se, it is not illogical either. Feeling is *alogical*—simply based on a different style of reaching decisions. Just as they do with sensation and intuition, people develop a preference for either thinking or feeling. Even though they can use either when required, people may be unsure of themselves when they rely on their blind side.

THINKING

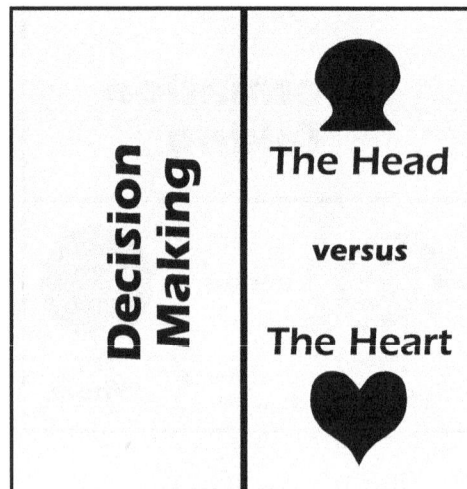

FEELING

PERSONALITY STYLE INSTRUMENT

Combining the two different ways of taking in information with the two different ways of making decisions defines the four personality styles:

STs enjoy the well-structured aspects of problem solving. Such people choose a certain alternative on the basis of a logical, impersonal analysis. ST people seek single answers to most questions and prefer the answers to be clearly right or wrong according to some quantitative assessment. It's not surprising, then, that ST persons are most confident dealing with details, facts, and well-established rules.

NTs enjoy looking at a complex situation from many different—global— perspectives. Such people are attracted to abstract discussions; they get bored with well-structured and routine problems, and they abhor details. NTs are especially good at creating theories, diagrams, and classification schemes to intellectually structure their world—which largely consists of ideas, possibilities, and conceptual frameworks.

SFs enjoy socializing. This activity satisfies their focus on the immediate experience as well as their need for being with friends. SF people are primarily concerned with the special needs of their fellow associates in the organization—rather than the technical or analytical aspects of the work. Their personal style and sensitivity enable them to feel how any decision might affect the quality of life for the organization's members.

NFs enjoy uncertainty and ambiguity. Such people prefer looking into the future and use their personal criteria for deciding what is important to consider. Such people thrive on dynamic complexity; they function best when there is a minimum of structure and when problems have not been defined yet. They are especially concerned about meaning, impact, and the future welfare of their organization and society.

Interpreting Your Scores

ST, NT, SF, and NF scores can vary between 0 and 40 (since there are ten items for each style with a scale from 0 to 4). Typically several (and in some cases all) of a person's scores fall between 15 and 25—the middle 50% of the distribution for each personality style (as represented by the **moderate shading** on the diagram). But it is not unusual for a person to have a score that falls between 0 and 14—the low 25% of the distribution for each style (as represented by the **mild shading** on the graph). Nor is it unusual for a person to have a score that falls between 26 and 40—the high 25% of the distribution for each style (as shown by the **dark shading** on the graph). For some people, in fact, two of their scores are moderate, one of their scores is high, while their remaining score is low—revealing a clear stylistic preference with an equally evident blind side.

The same explanation holds true for the average scores of work groups (or departments or the whole organization). The shape of the quadrangle conveys whether the work group (or organization) tends to approach all situations in the same manner (a specialist) or if a variety of styles are appreciated and utilized in the work environment (a generalist).

On the graph on the opposite page, a sample quadrangle is shown to illustrate a generalist profile for an organization. For this situation, all four average scores fall in the moderate range (between 15 and 25) and the quadrangle closely approaches the shape of a square—symbolizing the potential for fully appreciating and using all personality differences.

PERSONALITY STYLE INSTRUMENT

A Generalist Profile

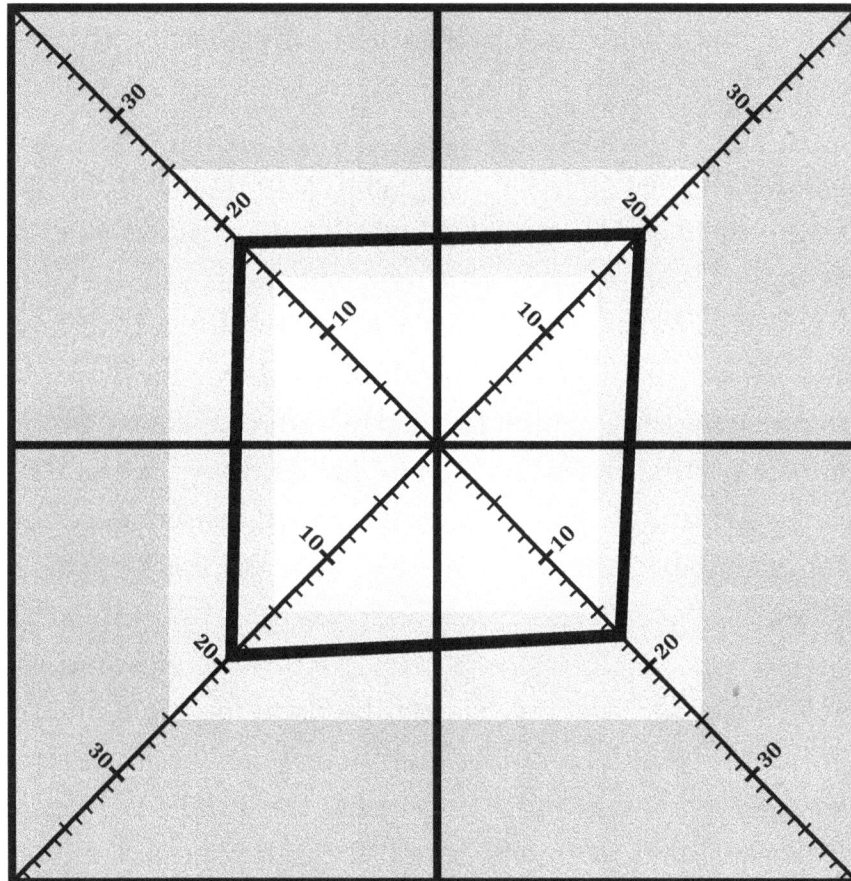

$\dfrac{18}{\textbf{ST}}$
AVERAGE

$\dfrac{19}{\textbf{NT}}$
AVERAGE

$\dfrac{19}{\textbf{SF}}$
AVERAGE

$\dfrac{17}{\textbf{NF}}$
AVERAGE

A quadrangle illustrating a specialist profile is shown on the opposite page. Note that only two averages (ST and NF) fall in the moderate range (15 to 25). The NT average is in the high range (26 to 40) while the SF average is in the low range (0 to 14). This particular distribution of styles results in a quadrangle whose shape varies significantly from a square—symbolizing the difficulty this organization will have in fully utilizing all personality differences.

The advantage of specialization is the ability to do one thing extremely well. In the case of an NT specialization, the organization would be able to concentrate on such matters as technological innovation and personal creativity. Such a focus might be especially useful in a high-technology organization—especially during periods of rapid growth. However, by not devoting the necessary attention to the day-to-day efficiency of the operations and the peculiar needs of the employees, this dominant NT style might very well result in numerous dysfunctional consequences in time—when, for example, the industry matures and the marketplace is more competitive.

This same sort of stylistic analysis can be done for any other specialist profile by amplifying the essential qualities of the dominant style while minimizing the potential contribution from the blind side. Thus, a high score in any quadrant represents a well-focused style best suited for its own unique piece of the organizational puzzle. The blind side, however, represents the one style most likely to be unappreciated, devalued, and, therefore, not fully utilized when its own special portion of a problem requires special attention.

PERSONALITY STYLE INSTRUMENT

A Specialist Profile

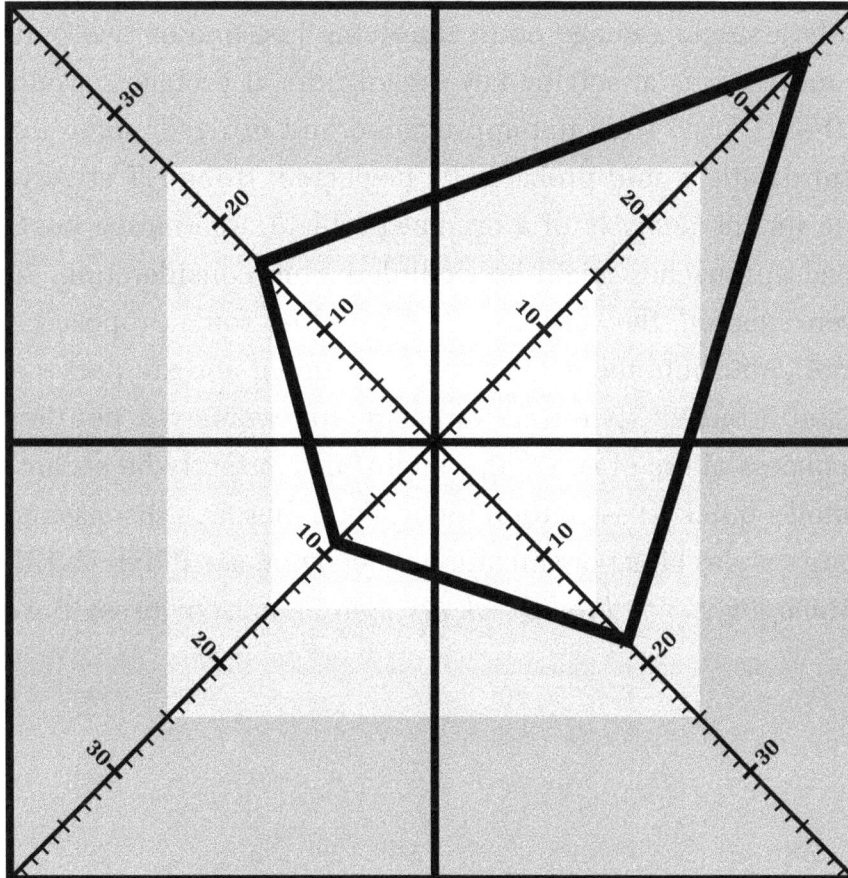

16
___
ST
AVERAGE

35
___
NT
AVERAGE

9
___
SF
AVERAGE

18
___
NF
AVERAGE

Managing Diversity

The ultimate challenge for individuals and organizations is to recognize all differences in style and use them explicitly for addressing complex problems. If any organization were to see its problems and opportunities from only a single vantage point (applying just one or two personality styles), most efforts at solving key organizational problems would likely fail. If the ST style were not appreciated and utilized, some important technical details would probably be neglected. If the NT style were not available for the analysis of a crucial problem, alternative possibilities and novel approaches might be excluded from consideration. If the SF style were ignored, the very people affected by some proposed solution might not contribute the necessary commitment and support to make it work. And if the NF style were put aside (or, worse yet, put down), the future success of the organization might inadvertently be exchanged for an ill-fated—quick fix—solution today. For a thorough discussion of how personality styles affect organizational behavior, see Ralph H. Kilmann's book, *Managing Beyond the Quick Fix*, San Francisco: Jossey-Bass, 1989.

Assessment Tools for the Eight Tracks
Distributed by Kilmann Diagnostics

Kilmann-Saxton Culture-Gap® Survey

Kilmanns Organizational Belief Survey

Kilmanns Time-Gap Survey

Kilmanns Team-Gap Survey

Organizational Courage Assessment

Kilmann-Covin Organizational Influence Survey

Kilmanns Personality Style Instrument

Plus the Online Version of the
Thomas-Kilmann Conflict Mode Instrument

Plus These Training and Development Tools
Work Sheets for Identifying and Closing Culture-Gaps
Work Sheets for Identifying and Closing Team-Gaps

And the Book That Fully Explains the Eight Tracks
Quantum Organizations

www.ingramcontent.com/pod-product-compliance
Lightning Source LLC
Chambersburg PA
CBHW081205270326
41930CB00014B/3311